CARTOONS

FROM THE GENERAL STRIKE

compiled and written by Michael Hughes

LONDON : EVELYN, ADAMS & MACKAY

First published in Britain in 1968 by Evelyn, Adams & Mackay Ltd
9 Fitzroy Square, London W1, and in the United States of America
by Augustus M Kelley Publishers, 24 East 22nd Street, New York,
NY 10010. Library of Congress Catalogue Card No. 68-24687
Printed at The Grange Press, Southwick, Sussex. Bound in England.

CARTOONS *FROM THE GENERAL STRIKE*

Acknowledgements

The Author and Publisher acknowledge the kindness of the following for permitting the reproduction of cartoons: Associated Newspapers Ltd pp 6, 11, 15, 53, *Glasgow Herald* p 17; Independent Labour Party p 23; *International Herald Tribune* p 19; International Publishing Corporation pp 35, 37; London Electrotype Agency pp 9, 45, 49; *Morning Star* Co-operative Society Ltd pp 55, 67; *News of the World* pp 39, 61; Odhams Press Ltd pp 13, 25, 57; *Pravda* p 31; © *Punch* pp 27, 33, 41, 43, 47, 51, 59, 63, 71; Victoria House Printing Company pp 21, 29.

The Author gratefully acknowledges assistance from the British Museum Newspaper Library (Colindale), the Hertfordshire County Library Service, the Library of the Labour Party, the National Union of Mineworkers and the Trades Union Congress.

Daily Graphic 28 April 1926

In 1925 the British coal industry was in an acute, deep-rooted depression. It was still the country's largest industry with a labour force of one million men, but from a prosperous period in the early 1920's it had declined to a condition in which 79 per cent. of pits were producing at a loss. In the first six months of 1926 the industry lost £2 million.

Its structure was archaic, with some 2,500 pits operated by 1,400 different owners. It was under-capitalised, machinery was antiquated, management was largely incompetent and obdurate. These native weaknesses were compounded when cheap Polish and German coal flooded the market after 1923, forcing world prices down. British coal was too weak to withstand foreign competition and lost heavily in export markets. The industry sank into crisis, forcing the miners into poverty.

The Conservative Government of the day was led by Stanley Baldwin, with Winston Churchill as Chancellor of the Exchequer. Baldwin had started Churchill on his eccentric career as Chancellor in 1924, since when the Gold Standard had occupied a central position in Churchill's thoughts and he had conceived an almost mystical desire for 'the restoration of a financial monarch to his rightful throne'. Against much advice he returned Britain to the Gold Standard in April 1925.

The immediate consequence of revaluation was to raise British export prices and coal, which relied heavily on foreign trade, was priced out of international markets (p. 6). The coal industry, particularly the men who worked in it, was thrust into disaster. As Keynes wrote in *The Economic Consequences of Mr Churchill,* the miners 'are the victims of the economic Juggernaut. They represent in the flesh the "fundamental adjustments" engineered by the Treasury and the Bank of England to satisfy the impatience of the City Fathers...'

The miners had usually suffered first when working conditions were under attack, and with coal the sick industry of Britain they were to be first again. The mine owners, 'about the least worthy element in the British community', knew only one response to the situation — force wages down and force hours up. In June they informed the Miners' Federation that existing wage agreements would be terminated at midnight on 31 July 1925. Simultaneously they announced new 'agreements' which cut miners' wages by 10-25 per cent., abolished the national minimum wage and increased the miner's working day.

The Miners' Federation angrily rejected these terms and sought and received full support for their stand from the General Council of the Trades Union Congress. The T.U.C. received pledges from several member unions that they would strike in sympathy with the miners. Thus encouraged the T.U.C. took the unprecedented step of calling a strike, and ordered a complete prohibition on the movement of coal from midnight on 31 July when the lock-out notices took effect.

With a national strike threatening, Baldwin overcame his distaste of government interference in 'private' affairs and appointed a Court of Inquiry. Throughout June and July he tried to bring owners and T.U.C. together, always with the proviso that the government was not prepared to give the coal industry any form of subsidy. No progress was made. On 29 July the Court of Inquiry recommended a settlement in favour of the miners. The owners rejected it and the miners were further convinced of the futility of negotiation. Baldwin persevered for a compromise but neither side would give an inch. 'Nowt doin' was the favourite phrase of Herbert Smith, the miners' President.

On the morning of Thursday, 30 July, Baldwin repeated and emphasised 'that the government can give no subsidy'. On the Thursday afternoon the T.U.C. dispatched orders to halt the nation's transport system from midnight on the Friday. King George V wrote in his diary 'I fear a strike now is inevitable at the end of the week. It will play the devil in the country.' On the Thursday evening the Cabinet met in stormy, emergency session. Baldwin left the meeting for the Ministry of Labour, where he announced to the half-believing miners what amounted to complete capitulation. The Government had decided, he said, to grant the coal industry a subsidy on profits and wages, which eventually cost £23 million; the

8

BY E. T. REED

RED GULCH COOK (*helping himself with impunity*): "So you're *the Governor of this State*, are yer! Wal, you've got the durned rummiest way of goin' about *governin'* as ever I saw! Pers'nally I don't make no complaints, but *ther' may be folks as will!*"

subsidy would operate until 1 May 1926, while a Royal Commission examined the coal industry; the subsidy would only be granted if the coal owners withdrew their notices.

Friday, 31 July 1925, when the British Government was vanquished by the Trades Union Congress, was christened 'Good Friday' by the *Daily Herald*; to the Tories it was known as 'Blackmail Friday' (p. 9), but to history and to those who saw strikes as a weapon of revolution it became known as 'Red Friday'.

'Red Friday' was a triumph for the miners and the General Council although the latter was uneasy at some of its militant allies. 'A. J. Cook on behalf of the T.U. left and Maxton and Wheatley on behalf of the Clyde talk about immediate revolution,' sourly recorded Beatrice Webb, 'whilst George Lansbury thunders threats of the immediate dissolution of the Capitalist civilisation.' And certainly many saw in 'Red Friday' a portent of capitalism's downfall. 'We stood together and won', said a miners' delegate, 'and we will win again and win again until the workers control the land'. This was not what the General Council intended, and many of its members found such sentiments disturbing.

They also disturbed Ramsay Macdonald, the leader of the Labour Party and arch-schlerotic in that hardening of the radical arteries which was upon the party. By 1925 Labour was experiencing that need for respectability, moderation and the approval of the middle classes which is now characteristic, and Macdonald voiced official reaction when he said of 'Red Friday': 'the Government has simply handed over the appearance, at any rate, of victory to the very forces that sane, well considered, thoroughly examined Socialism feels probably to be its greatest enemy'.

The Conservative Party and its press agreed with him. To them 'Red Friday' was a victory for the revolutionaries, a humiliating defeat for public order and constitutional rule. They raged against the government's surrender, and attacked Baldwin as venomously as the trade unions (p. 11). The Government's compromise, made from weakness but also

"SITUATIONS VACANT."

from some recognition of the miner's plight, was whipped up by a fearful press into the Fall of the Bastille, and when newspapers cried 'it must not happen again' they were imagining the rumble of tumbrilos when the subsidy ran out.

But to the Miners' Federation 'Red Friday' did not foreshadow Armageddon or the dictatorship of the proletariat. They had experienced too many fruitless enquiries to expect much of the Royal Commission, and they knew the mood and obstinacy of the mine owners. Herbert Smith expressed widespread apprehension when he opened a Delegate Conference in August by saying 'We have no need to glorify about a victory. It is only an armistice . . .', and the miners knew that what followed the lifting of the armistice on 1 May 1926 would decide whose was the victory.

This was precisely the Government's attitude. Churchill, speaking publicly in December 1925, said of 'Red Friday': 'We therefore decided to postpone the crisis in the hope of averting, or . . . coping effectually with it when the time came'. And Baldwin later wrote 'We were not ready'. Immediately after 'Red Friday' the Government began preparations to ensure that next time they would be ready.

Since the Great War some sections of government and labour had been convinced that a major showdown between the two was inevitable. Syndicalist ideas were again in favour on the left, and the belief that a massive strike could defeat the government and usher in a workers' Valhalla had many takers (p. 13). In both government and industry there were many who saw the growth of the left and the strengthening of trade-union power as a menace to the nation, and they hungered for a conflict in which the left and the unions would be irretrievably damaged.

Both ideologies were equally romantic and illusory, but it was in response to such pressures that an Emergency Powers Act had been passed in 1920, and it was under the mantle of this measure, and influenced by a revival of the beliefs which had brought it about, that the Government devised its plans against another 'Red Friday'.

The Committee appointed for this task made preparations

Daily Herald 28 July 1925

13

as if to fight a bloody war. They divided the country into ten areas 'for the purposes of industrial strife', each one under a Civil Commissioner who was generally a junior minister. Eighty-eight Voluntary Service Committees were appointed, headed by 'reliable' people of the peer-of-the-realm, retired-general, master-of-foxhounds variety. In the event of a strike the Commissioners, through the V.S.C.'s, were to co-ordinate local services of all kinds and generally keep going the life of the nation. If violence or strife occurred the Commissioners were authorised to exercise all of the Government's powers to preserve order and protect loyal subjects. In effect, in certain circumstances the Government planned to replace or subordinate locally elected government with extra-constitutional bodies directed from Whitehall, a step infinitely more revolutionary than anything contemplated by the unions. It is worth noting that British governments have made similar plans on only two subsequent occasions – when threatened by Nazi Germany and when threatened by nuclear holocaust. Adolf Hitler, the Bomb and the British Striker.

There was also semi-unofficial preparation in the form of a body called the 'Organisation for the Maintenance of Supplies'. Founded by a number of eminent ex-public servants – a one-time Viceroy of India, a retired Admiral of the Fleet, a few Generals, etc. – the O.M.S. was the most distinguished and cultured strike-breaking organisation of all time. Backed by 'certain funds . . . (which) have been placed by a few patriotic citizens at the disposal of the Council . . .' its object was to register and classify those citizens of all classes and either sex 'who are prepared to render voluntary assistance in maintaining the supply of food, water, and fuel' in the event of a strike. Established in September 1925 by private initiative but with probable Government connivance the O.M.S. was a slightly comic body : about 100,000 people enrolled in it, from either political conviction or a desire to drive buses and trains. In several towns the British Fascists volunteered as a body, sometimes to be accepted, sometimes not. When the Strike came the O.M.S. turned out to be a damp squib, but

Star 3 October 1925

during the armistice it undoubtedly dramatised the strike issue, aroused a slumbering populace and, however genteelly, marked out the borders of class warfare (p. 15).

Government preparations were massive, extremely thorough and deadly serious, and had half the energy expended been directed towards solving the mining dispute the industry's problems would have been over. By May 1926 the Government had built up a disciplined organisation throughout the land, authorised to assume government if necessary; it had at its disposal about 200,000 vehicles through a subsidy (!) agreement with private operators; there were coal stocks to last five months; the number of special constables had been increased from 98,000 to 226,000 and a reserve of 18,000 men had been created; military, naval and police forces had been briefed to occupy or guard docks, power stations and telephone exchanges and to maintain road, rail and water communications. There were to be no more 'Blackmail Fridays'.

And the T.U.C. and the Miners' Federation while these plans were being laid? Between October 1925 and the eve of the General Strike the T.U.C. did not meet once to plan support for the miners. Its Special Industrial Committee held a watching brief, but watch was about all it did. Of plans to feed the strikers, to develop communications, organise transport, prepare publicity, plan a newspaper — there were none. What little activity there was comprised words not deeds as speakers, or agitators if you preferred it, caught the headlines with their appeals, threats and boasts. Chief of these was A. J. Cook, a self-confessed 'humble follower of Lenin', who was Secretary of the Miners' Federation.

It seems that each generation produces one trade-union leader who develops a kind of reverse-charisma and becomes a repository of middle-class fears and prejudices. A. J. Cook, as he toured the coalfields exhorting the miners to organise, fulfilled this role in the mid-20's as the best-hated man in England. From his youth in the South Wales pits Cook had retained a profound, emotional feeling for the wretchedness

16   *Bulletin (Glasgow) 15 June 1926*

and suffering of the mining families, and his hatred of those who caused and profitted from their condition was almost tangible. He was a magnificent orator who could bring crowds, and himself, to tears, and he had often brought whole pits out with his impassioned appeals. He was utterly selfless and the miners, in a very real way, loved him.

The mine-owners did not love him. One of them wrote, with unintended tribute, 'Cook is a typical demagogue, and as such is a coiner of apt phrases such as, for example, "Not a penny off the pay, not a second on the day" – a sentence which by incessant employment has achieved the rank of a slogan, and has so implanted its policy in the minds of the general mine workers as to have become almost a creed' (p. 17). It was said of him that 'He had great heart but little head', because he often let his passionate belief in the justice of his cause overrun the credibility of his position. 'I don't care a hang for any government, any army or navy', he said in 1925, 'They can come along with their bayonets. Bayonets don't cut coal.' . . . 'We have already beaten, not only the employers, but the strongest government in modern times'. . . . 'We won last time and we'll do it again, but next time no subsidy will buy off our terms'. To the Nottinghamshire miners he said 'We are organising. We are building our food supplies. Our hearts are strong, and we will beat Churchill, the Government, the employers and the O.M.S.' 'We' were doing nothing of the sort, but the newspapers seized on such statements to frighten the middle classes.

Cook angered his moderate colleagues on the General Council almost as much as he alarmed his opponents, and this when the moderates were much stronger than before 'Red Friday'. Prominent among these was J. H. Thomas, MP, of the Railwaymen, o companion of 'press lords, noble dukes and gentlemen'. Thomas once said 'I don't complain when I see myself in my evening clothes – that draws attention to my importance'. To Cook he was the archetypal labour sell-out and he christened him 'the boss's monkey'. Thomas disliked Cook with equal vigour and never tried to conceal it. 'My regret is that a great organisation like the Miners' Federation

should day after day have its cause ruined by the childish outbursts of its secretary' he wrote in the *Daily Herald.* And again 'All those who happen to know most about events are praying that he will take a rest and so render more lasting service to the cause of the workers.'

Cook and Thomas represented in extreme form the divisions within the General Council, although in calling for negotiation the influential Thomas more typified majority opinion. The T.U.C. did not want a strike for it knew from direct experience the suffering and cost inevitably involved. It knew what a tremendous gamble a *general* strike was and the awful consequences which would stem from failure, and it was fully aware of the government's preparations against one. 'Red Friday' it regarded as a fluke which had not tested the workers' solidarity, and it had grave doubts about welding many proud, iconoclastic unions into one cohesive strike force. Sadly it allowed the wish to become the deed, and led by those like Thomas who argued that preparations for a strike would arouse the nation against them, the General Council made no plans to support the miners. Like lambs they awaited the Report of the Royal Commission, fooling themselves that it might offer a solution to the coal industry's problems.

Baldwin had appointed the Royal Commission on 25 September under Sir Herbert Samuel, one-time Home Secretary and lately Governor of Palestine. The other members were Sir William Beveridge, economist, ex-civil servant and Director of the London School of Economics, General Sir Herbert Lawrence, partner in Glyn, Mills, the bankers, and Kenneth Lee, a Midland Bank director and chairman of Tootal, Lee, Broadhurst, the cotton manufacturers.

There were no representatives of the owners or the miners on the Commission, nor indeed anyone with experience of the coal industry. 'What would they say', asked Cook 'if *I* appointed a Commission on the Stock Exchange out of a plate-layer, a shop assistant and an engine driver?'. But that was the point – Baldwin intended that 'fresh minds should be

THE EXTRA HAND IS TAKEN ON

(The miners contended that it was during the last hour of the working day that accidents occurred – M. H.)

brought to bear' by people who were neutral in the dispute. They were, in truth, as neutral as an establishment politician, a liberal economist, a financier and a banker/manufacturer could be expected to be.

The Commission reported on 10 July. Its Report set out the arguments for nationalisation as a cure for the industry's ills but it rejected them; it did, however, recommend State ownership of the royalities from coal. It judged the subsidy 'indefensible' and 'never to be repeated'. It supported the national minimum wage. It recommended the *voluntary* amalgamation of small pits. It called for better employer-labour relations and made suggestions for profit sharing, family allowances, more pithead baths, holidays with pay 'when prosperity returns', improved housing and incentive schemes.

It was when the Report came to deal with the part the miner would play in the industry's renascence that it ceased to be realistic, for it recommended that the miner take a cut in wages or else work longer hours for the same pay. The miner's 7-hour day, bitterly fought for and guaranteed by Parliament, was a violently emotional matter and this recom-mendation was bound to cause an outcry (p. 21). It asked the miners, in effect, to make profound sacrifices in the present for undefined benefits in the future. They were invited to accept the owners' promises of rationalisation and improved welfare 'when economic circumstances allow', in exchange for an immediate reduction in pay or longer hours.

This is what 'Red Friday' had been fought over, and were they expected to renounce that victory for pie in the sky? Just after the Report was issued a friend said to the Miners' leaders that it gave them two-thirds of what they wanted. 'It gives us three-quarters', said Cook, 'and we can't accept it'. The reply typified the miners' reactions, which were admirably summarised in Cook's 1925 slogan, now to be reminted and to sweep the coalfields as a capsule statement of the miners' demands 'Not a penny off the pay. Not a second on the day'.

The owners were equally intransigent. They were adamant

that the national minimum wage must be replaced by direct agreements, that wages must be reduced, that hours must be increased. (If accepted, their demands would have plunged hundreds of thousands down to pre-1914 wage levels: would, for example, have reduced a Durham miner's pay by 18s. 3d. a week, would have dropped a South Wales hewer from 78s. to 45s. 10d. a week.) They were equally immovable on refusing to discuss future re-organisation, for until their demands had been met and the consequences observed, how could they, as honourable men, make promises which they might not be able to keep? Indeed.

It was tragic that the continual conflict which had riven the coalfields during the century had taught the owners nothing but stubbornness. J. L. Garvin wrote of them in *The Observer* 'No responsible body of men has ever seemed more lacking in the human touch', while Lord Birkenhead, who was in the Cabinet, wrote 'It would be possible to say without exaggeration that the miners' leaders were the stupidest men in England if we had not had frequent occasion to meet the owners'.

The Government had accepted the entire Samuel report and Baldwin had promised legislation to give it effect. His condition, however, was that both sides should likewise accept it for he would not consider legislation which either the owners or the miners opposed. It was an invitation to deadlock, an invitation for owners and miners to veto each other on wages and re-organisation. This was Baldwin's famous 'neutrality' — 'I do not favour one side or the other. I wish only that they should agree between themselves'. With the miners already on starvation wages, and the owners not unreluctant for a strike and contemplating lock-out notices, it was neutrality as between a drowning man and the sea.

Throughout the first three weeks of April Baldwin maintained his neutrality, offering only exhortations and platitudes (p. 25) while no doubt tying up the loose ends of the Government's anti-strike plans. Half-hearted attempts at compromise were made: the Miners' Federation met the Mining Association, the T.U.C.'s Industrial Committee met both, the Labour Party

joined in, but no progress was made. Had the Government or the owners tabled even tentative proposals for re-organising the industry there might have been some, for the Industrial Committee saw this as a face-saver, but the owners refused to consider the future and the Government would accept no responsibility in the matter. At a meeting on 13 April it was apparent that negotiation would at that stage lead nowhere. The owners therefore returned to their districts and posted notices at most pitheads terminating existing contracts on 30 April, to coincide with the end of the subsidy. For the second time in nine months the miners were threatened with lock-out.

This at least provoked activity and Baldwin stirred himself to call a meeting for 22 April, just one week before the notices expired. This achieved nothing, the owners refused to with-draw the notices and inflexibly restated their demands. 'Nowt doin',' said Herbert Smith. 'Not a penny off. Not a second on,' said Arthur Cook. The miners were also resigned to a strike. The Industrial Committee had slightly weakened in its support of the miners, hoping that a small compromise on wages would secure firm proposals on re-organisation from the Government. But with the owners wanting unconditional surrender and the Government refusing to get involved they supported the miners without qualification. The last week of April witnessed feverish, fruitless activity. Government, owners, Miners, Industrial Committee met in permutation. The miners called a delegate conference, the T.U.C. sum-moneded its General Council to London. Still deadlock. It was in this *last* week, on the Tuesday, that Ernest Bevin and a colleague got down to the first draft of the T.U.C.'s strike plan.

On Friday, 30 April, the Industrial Committee met with the Government throughout the day. Hopes of a settlement were high as a thousand trade-union executives sat the day out in the Memorial Hall, waiting for news. To pass the time they sang hymns and music-hall songs, recited patriotic verse and played pontoon – a respectable, subdued gathering of ordi-nary British workmen, not bellicose, certainly not revolu-tionary. Throughout the day in the House of Commons the

UNDER WHICH FLAG?

JOHN BULL. "ONE OF THESE TWO FLAGS HAS GOT TO COME DOWN—AND IT WON'T
BE MINE."

miners, the Industrial Committee and some senior Labour M.P.s had argued desperately for a settlement. At 8.30 p.m. a compromise from the owners was announced: they were prepared to accept a national minimum wage if it was set at the 1921 level and if the miners would work an eight-hour day for at least three-and-a-half years: the 'compromise' meant an extra hour's work and a wage cut of 13 per cent. It was intolerable but it was not rejected out of hand. Would Baldwin make any concrete proposals about future re-organisation? He would not. He was willing to arrange for 'an authoritative enquiry' into the problems, but he would not himself make or accept any proposals or promises. The trade unionists persisted. J. H. Thomas of the Railwaymen, Cook's arch-enemy and a moderate of moderates, later said: 'My friends, when the verbatim reports are written, I suppose my usual critics will say that Thomas was almost grovelling, and it is true. In all my long experience – and I have conducted many negotiations – I say to you – and my colleagues will bear testimony to it – I never begged and pleaded like I begged and pleaded all day today'. During the time the parties were locked in negotiation several things happened outside the House of Commons of which the trade unionists were not aware. In the afternoon the Government sent to all Local Authorities a circular which listed the Civil Commissioners and their staff and called the regional organisations to a state of readiness. In the early evening they called a special meeting of the Privy Council at which the King signed a Proclamation declaring a State of Emergency, which gave wide powers to the Government without reference to Parliament. The Organisation for the Maintenance of Supplies handed over its membership records to the Government, and on the Saturday afternoon O.M.S. posters appeared throughout the country calling for more volunteers. The Government and the O.M.S. had mobilised.

In the Commons the trade unionists still sought for a concession which would get them off the hook, but Baldwin had abandoned any pretence of being a neutral arbitrator. He was now demanding that the miners accept the owners, terms in

In answer to the "British Gazette"

UNDER WHICH FLAG?

Lansbury's Labour Weekly 22 May 1926

exchange for yet another inquiry and some vague promises of future legislation. 'I want to see the horse I am going to mount,' said Herbert Smith. The meeting broke up.

On 1 May, in the morning, the General Council obtained agreement from the Miners' Federation that they would hand over their powers in any strike to the T.U.C. At lunchtime Congress convened for the awesome decision. Bevin opened by outlining the Council's proposals for action in support of the miners. They were vague, but the crucial one was that 'certain trades and undertakings shall cease work as and when required by the General Council', and the time when they would cease was midnight on Monday, 3 May. A ballot was taken and there were 3,653,527 votes for the strike, 49,911 against. Delegates were then asked if they would hand over 'the conduct of the dispute' to the T.U.C. This was an unprecedented request for it meant giving the T.U.C. access to trade union funds, giving it power to call out or return their members to work, giving it power to extend or terminate the strike on its own terms. Almost unanimously the delegates voted these powers to the T.U.C.

The precise extent of these powers was later to cause profound bitterness between Miners' and T.U.C. but at the time it was a great decision, nobly taken. After singing the 'Red Flag' the delegates dispersed to their districts to lead, from incredibly unprepared positions, the greatest struggle of workingmen since Chartism. That afternoon Ernest Bevin had spelled out what was expected of them : 'We look upon your "yes" as meaning that you have placed your all upon the alter of this great Movement, and having placed it there, even if every penny goes, if every asset goes, history will ultimately write up that it was a magnificent generation that was pre-pared to do it rather than see the miners driven down like slaves . . . I rely, in the name of the General Council, on every man and every woman in that grade to fight for the soul of Labour and the salvation of the miners . . .'

The events of Saturday evening and Sunday were a farce which degenerated into tragedy. Briefly, the General Council

Pravda 4 May 1926

had restarted negotiations with the Government, a formula had been devised which offered a good chance of success, when an astonished General Council discovered that it could not be approved as the Miners' Executive had left for the coalfields. The Executive was hurriedly recalled, and while its members journeyed to London the Cabinet met to receive a reply on the formula. Unfortunately the General Council forgot to inform the Cabinet of the Miners' absence; the Cabinet waited for the Council and when it didn't arrive angrily broke up in a strong anti-T.U.C. mood.

At 11 p.m. negotiations were again in progress at Downing Street. Hopes of agreement were high when a Secretary appeared and announced that the Prime Minister wished to see them. Four of them went downstairs where a solemn Baldwin waited in the Cabinet Room. He handed them a letter. 'Goodbye, I am sorry', he said. 'This is the end'. The letter said that the Government was alarmed 'not only that specific instructions have been sent . . . to carry out a general strike . . . but that overt acts have already taken place, including gross interference with the freedom of the press'. This referred to some workers on the *Daily Mail* who had that evening refused to print a violent, anti-union editorial for Monday's paper. Their action was entirely personal and the T.U.C. was in no way involved, but the Government had chosen to see it as the opening shots of the Strike.

A bewildered General Council immediately drafted a repudiation of the 'overt acts' and took it below. To their astonishment the Cabinet Room was in darkness: The Cabinet had left, Baldwin had gone to bed. The Government's interpretation of the *Daily Mail* incident made the General Strike unavoidable — an interpretation which *Pravda,* for rather different reasons, chose to make (p. 31). It was an incredible reason for setting a nation to war with itself and it indicated that Baldwin had lost ground to those in the Cabinet who wanted a strike. The T.U.C. had always sought for compromise, but with a settlement almost within reach this had been refused. It must now fight a battle it had never wanted. Twenty-three hours later the General Strike began.

REPERCUSSIONS OF THE STRIKE.

Maid. "WHAT WILL MADAM WEAR?"
Mistress. "WELL, I REALLY DON'T KNOW. WHAT DOES ONE WEAR FOR A STRIKE?"

'Tuesday, 4 May, started with the workers answering the call. What a wonderful response! What loyalty!! What solidarity!!! From John O'Groats to Land's End the workers answered the call to arms to defend us, to defend the brave miner in his fight for a living wage.' That was A. J. Cook, exhilarant at the response to the strike, which had far exceeded expectations. The T.U.C. had called out only the 'first line' industries — the railwaymen, the transport workers, the iron, steel and heavy chemical men, the printers, and building workers not employed on housing or hospitals. With the exception of three small unions they had solidly obeyed, and the one million miners who had been locked out were voluntarily joined by one-and-a-half million others. The sacrifices of these men needs emphasising. In 1926 unemployment was high, wages were low and savings non-existent. To strike meant an immediate loss of earnings and probable loss of job. Yet millions freely decided to bring hardship on themselves and their families, without knowing how hard or how long it would be. And they did this not to profit themselves but to support the miners.

On the morning of Tuesday, 5 May, the nation awoke to a transformed Britain. The cities discovered it first — the silence. No buses or trains ran, the factories were still, nothing moved on the docks. On the railways the stoppage was almost 100 per cent. Of 15,062 drivers employed by the L.M.S. only 207 reported for work; of 14,143 firemen, only 62; of 9,979 guards, only 153. The nation's railways had stopped.

The transport workers were likewise solid. The London Omnibus Company owned 3,933 buses. None of these left the garages on the first day, and even with O.M.S. drivers only 526 were later to take the road. Only 15 of London's underground trains ran, and the trams were at a standstill. At the London docks no ships were unloaded or cargoes moved until by O.M.S. volunteers under protection of armed soldiers. And from the provinces came news of a similar solidarity. There were blackspots, particularly among provincial busmen, but in most places a fantastic 90 per cent answered

the T.U.C.'s call. In George Lansbury's words: 'In mining village and agricultural township, in great cities and small towns, all the Workers who count in the business of life just stood still, folded their arms, and with scarcely any disorder refused to move'.

If the workers' response had astonished that of their opponents was predictable. In their journal, *The Coal and Iron News,* the owners blamed the stoppage entirely on the miners, for rejecting their terms, 'the generosity of which was more even than the men could have reasonably expected'. They would accept no responsibility for precipitating the Strike by the lock-out, for the notices at the pitheads 'were simply schedules of terms under which the men may continue to work. Any body of miners who presented themselves at their regular pits on these terms could obtain employment'. For 13 per cent. under for an extra hour.

The *Daily Mail,* whose belligerency had partly precipitated the Strike, responded with unrestrained provocation. Its eve-of-strike leader had compared the legitimate, elected government with a 'second, lawless, uncontrollable, revolutionary government' – it meant the T.U.C. 'Two governments', it said, 'cannot exist in the same capital. One must destroy the other or surrender to the other'. The *Mail* was one of the few national dailies to enjoy wide distribution during the Strike. It distorted the vision and hardened the mood of many with its demand for unconditional surrender and its talk of 'revolutionary movements', 'warfare', and 'Russian inspired plots'.

The Government's response began on Sunday evening with a coded telegram, 'Action', to the Civil Commissioners, and preparations were well advanced when the Strike started. Large numbers of troops were moved into London and the provincial centres, supplied with 'teargas, harmless but temporarily paralysing, to curb angry mobs, rather than take the fatal step of using bullets'. Warships took up station off several ports and in the rivers Tyne, Humber and Clyde. The Army took over the distribution of food, the Navy worked the docks and distributed petrol. The Civil Commissioners began

37

organising their army of volunteers, reservists and specials into the jobs vacated by the strikers.

Typical of the Government's thoroughness was a massive milk-distribution centre which sprang up in Hyde Park. Equipped with its own telephone network and water supplies it contained offices for the railway companies serviced with gas, water and electricity, canteens, rest and recreation rooms, and a library. From here thousands of lorries fetched and carried food and milk to the people of London, brilliantly organised and co-ordinated. True to the principles of its creators the milk pool made £73,000 profit.

The first day at Strike Headquarters was a shambles. The T.U.C. was almost completely unprepared for the largest-ever strike and its efforts to direct the fortunes of two million strikers were ludicrous. The small H.Q. staff, without a plan to work from or a formulated strategy to guide it, was overwhelmed by an avalanche of reports, committees, delegations, pressmen, photographers, telephone calls and rumours. While the Government's preparations moved smoothly forward the T.U.C. was in turmoil. The situation was retrieved by an incisive Bevin, who established a Strike Organisation Committee and several specialist committees responsible for publicity, intelligence, public services, the issue of permits and the publication of the *British Worker.* Through these the Strike Organisation Committee began to exert some control.

Outside Headquarters it was as bad. Strike machinery was almost non-existent and was hurriedly improvised by trades councils, unionists, local Labour Parties and sometimes local councillors. Strike Committees were set up for most areas to relieve distress, organise meetings, duplicate news-sheets, picket, issue permits and distribute the *British Worker.* With no prior briefing or clear idea of their role they set about organising the strikers and maintaining certain public services in a country which was at a standstill. In most areas they were extremely successful. They received instructions from London which were sometimes contradictory, often unintelligble and generally late, but they muddled through. They had to contend with large meetings, mass pickets,

News of the World 13 June 1926

angry crowds, belligerent policemen, Fascist demonstrations, vehicle wrecking and blacklegs. Not least they had to contend with the Strike Organisation Committee which, determined to prevent local control from slipping into the hands of the Communists, insisted that all their actions should be checked out with Headquarters. This produced infinite delays and lost opportunities and contributed most to their difficulties. When the Government rejected the T.U.C.'s offer to assist with food supplies the General Council decided to establish its own licensing system for road transport. To the Strike Committees fell the job of implementing this, which they did with immense satisfaction and varying efficiency. Vehicles were stopped by road blocks and human barriers and if not carrying food they were turned back; those allowed through had to display specially printed stickers: 'By permission of the T.U.C.' and this visible display of the Committees' power gave great satisfaction. Some Committees had to contend with violence and extreme provocation. The young Nye Bevan, cutting his teeth as Chairman of the Tredegar Council of Action, was told by the local police chief 'If there's any trouble here we'll have the place running with blood', a fairly common threat. In a few places where trouble from the Fascists, the O.M.S. or the police seemed certain 'Workers Defence Corps' were formed. There are no reports of their ever going into battle, but Abe Moffat has given us a picture of one such 'special platoon' in Fifeshire, carrying defensive weapons, led by a Great War veteran and drilling in the streets, 'a really splendid sight, well disciplined and determined to stand their ground'. On the Scottish coalfields it was as well to prepare for a fight.

The Strike Committees were a remarkable example of improvisation and self-help. They grew from nothing into co-ordinated, disciplined bodies firmly controlling their areas. They kept the Strike orderly and good humoured and they gave ordinary workers a new appreciation and confidence of their abilities.

During the months of pre-strike negotiations the public had by and large supported the miners, partly from a British love

Punch 26 May 1926

"My husband lost frightfully through the strike, so if I get a really *good* hat it might cheer him up a lot."

of the underdog and partly from an ingrained sense of justice which had taught them that the goodie should always win. General Council members had spent some time deliberating whether this sympathy would hold during the Strike or whether an enraged citizenry would tear the strikers limb from limb. They had concluded that most of the working class would support them, that the middle class would split but be mainly against and that the upper class would oppose as powerfully as it could. Their brilliant prescience was confirmed, but even the General Council could not have forseen the extremes of fear and comradeship, farce and nobility, the hysteria, the emnity, the humour and tolerance, the sheer bloody-mindedness which the Strike discovered in the British people.

It was genuinely believed in some quarters, upper rather than lower, that the General Strike was a revolutionary plot aimed at the overthrow of the British constitution. In some versions it was financed from Moscow, so that when Russian miners sent money for the strike fund the T.U.C. hurriedly and ostentatiously declined the gift (p. 39). The *Daily Mail* continually implied this, Churchill ranted in similar terms, *John Bull* talked of a striker's victory which 'would put us under a tyranny as intolerable as any tyranny of kings or oligarchy against which the nation has rebelled in the past'. Arnold Bennett noted in his diary after dining at the Reform Club: 'General opinion that the strike would be short but violent. Bloodshed expected next week'. Fear of violence was widespread. The future Lady Furness was met off a boat in strike-bound Southampton by Viscount Furness. They climbed into the Rolls and as they moved off for London 'Duke . . . pulled a revolver out of his pocket. "Now", he said, "I'd like to see any bastard stop this car".' In greenest Hampshire one gentleman 'recalled firearms from his game keepers, placed his forester's tools under lock and key' and under cover of darkness he and his butler 'buried the entire contents of his wine and spirits cellar' in the shrubbery. Whether to save the drink, or himself from drunken strikers, was not reported.

GISY.

LEGS AND THE STRIKE.

BEFORE.   AFTER.

It was not only the upper classes who feared. The Home Secretary, Joynson-Hicks, had aroused considerable anxiety by his intemperate appeals for special constables to 'release the regular police for perhaps sterner work', while the movement of armed troops and warships when the strike started led many to expect Government inspired violence.

The Baroness de T'Serclaes, who had won distinction in the Great War by establishing advance nursing-posts in the front lines, entered 'enemy territory' – working-class Poplar – and set up a nursing station in an empty shop. A large, unfriendly crowd gathered outside and despite the Red Cross flag was threatening and abusive. The gathering was explained when a police inspector arrived and requested that the Baroness and her nurses depart before violence broke out – 'the people are convinced that you have been sent by the army. They think it is planning an attack on civilians and that you are here to look after the wounded troops'. There *was* violence, although set against the magnitude of the Strike it was insignificant. In Scotland, Wales and London police baton charges led to street fighting, in London and the large cities stones were thrown and buses were wrecked. There were two attempts to derail trains and there were hundreds of skirmishes arising out of public meetings and picketing. In Doncaster a fight with the police earned 84 strikers three months each in jail; in Newcastle there were hundreds of casualties when the police brutally charged a peaceful crowd. The number of violent incidents was considerable, but out of approximately three million strikers the final figure for prosecutions was only 1,386 for violence and 1,760 for incitement. Lady Diana Cooper, in her autobiography *Light of Common Day* records that she 'could hear the tumbrilos rolling and heads sneezing into the baskets, and yet and yet, the English could not be like that'. Her second sentiment was shared by most people, and when the Strike came they were not like that at all.

The General Strike has been described as 'a nine day Bank Holiday', which well expresses much of its spirit, for to a

OUR PLUS-FORCE !

None but the brave deserved the fare!

By Blam

large proportion of the population it was not a revolutionary threat or a challenge to the constitution, but a lark – a holiday with entertainment provided free. With transport at a halt, particularly in London, it was difficult to reach work, and those that didn't feel very strongly about this stayed at home. For the others every means of private transport, however old, however exotic, was pressed into service, and the solid mass of jammed traffic which was central London was itself an entertainment for an age in which a traffic jam was still a novelty. If you couldn't drive you joined the long columns of walkers which converged on central London like the spokes of a wheel (p. 43) ; these developed a comradeship which for many recalled going up to the Somme. If you were lucky, or pretty, you were offered a lift, for motorists developed a never-to-be-repeated concern for pedestrians and offered the hospitality of their vehicles to anyone going their way (p. 51). Cars were bedecked with flags, stickers and notices of humorous intent – SEE LONDON BY TRAFFIC JAM, PEACE NOW AND FOREVER HOLD YOUR STRIKE, and the crowds cheered these perilously overloaded vehicles as the last typist was sardined aboard and they chugged along Piccadilly towards the suburbs. There were also the buses, driven by learners – very infrequent, and uncertain of where they were going or whether they would arrive – but worth waiting for if you liked the idea of riding with police escorts and having bricks thrown at you. In London cheerful crowds strolled the pavements out of boredom or curiosity, stared at the township which had sprung up in Hyde Park, watched Churchill's provocative armoured cars pass or clustered around the radio shops to hear the news bulletins.

At the Oval cricket ground Surrey were playing the Australians after the Cabinet had decreed that the match should be played in the interests of good feelings between classes. Buckingham Palace announced that the first two Courts of the Season would *not* be cancelled, come revolution or not, which *The Bystander* thought to be a deadly blow against the 'rabid revolutionaries' who 'forget the amount of employment which depends upon such functions'. And those

Lady (sweetly). "Do you go to Park Lane?"
Volunteer Conductor (gallantly). "Well, we don't, but I've no doubt we could."

who listened daily for the mob pounding on their door, realised that God was still in his heaven when a spokesman for the Great Western Railway soothed public disquiet by announcing that none of their horses had missed a meal since the strike began. The heroes of the Strike for the press, the cartoonists and those not actually taking part were the volunteers, the men and women who came forward to take over the jobs of absent strikers and who kept the country's essential services going.

The Government had anticipated the need to replace strikers and had connived at the O.M.S. with this in mind, but when the Strike was so unexpectedly effective – and the O.M.S. so ineffective where technical services were concerned – the Government made repeated appeals for volunteers. Thousands answered the call, were given rudimentary training and were set to unload ships, drive buses and trains, carry messages, stoke power stations, feed their colleagues and attend to the hundreds of other jobs which needed to be done in a society deprived of its muscle-power. A surprisingly high proportion of the volunteers were undergraduates, who in plus-fours and the newly fashionable pullovers became the public's favourites (p. 45). Many colleges encouraged students to volunteer for the Government and a complaint was laid against University College, London, which was denied, that students were encouraged with promises that 'their services would be remembered and taken into consideration during examinations'. Redbrick as well as Oxbridge supplied their quota of volunteers, staff as well as students. Undergraduates did voluntary work of every kind, from manual to intellectual, but it was on the buses that they won the public's heart.

Driving buses during the Strike was the most vulnerable form of blacklegging, and more violence and arrests stemmed from efforts to stop buses than from any other cause. The strikers picketed the garages in great numbers and few drivers managed to get their vehicles beyond the garage doors. A driver who did was lucky if he was stopped at the first road junction, politely asked to descend and his vehicle im-

A TRUE INCIDENT.

THE PICKET (*to the "Special"*): "D'ye mean to say you were a Rear-Admiral before you took on this job? Blimy! Wot a come down!"

DRAWN BY HERT THOMAS.

mobilised by the removal of a vital part. More likely his vehicle would be a target for the striker's bricks and bottles and all his windows would be smashed. The driver was usually protected by a screen of wire-netting around his cab and possibly a brace of policemen riding alongside, but if the policemen were so unkind as to depart the bus would soon be stopped, off would come the wire-netting, down would climb the driver to trudge back to headquarters, and the bus would be over-turned, immobilised or would disappear into the East End, not to reappear until the Strike was over. There were parts of Glasgow, Liverpool and the East End of London where buses never dared go, but volunteers were not generally sent to drive in the dangerous areas; when they were they survived the skirmishes cheerfully and usually without harm. Mostly they drove in 'government' areas where their antics inspired a fund of anecdotes, amusement and affection. They set a style for decorating their buses with notices and slogans for the amusement of passengers and to demonstrate their wit and bravado :

Here we are again, Ladies of normal size 3d.

I have no pane, dear Mother, now.

A brick in the hand is worth two in the bus.

Don't shoot we're out of season.

The driver of this bus is a student of Guy's Hospital. The conductor of this bus is a student of Guy's. Anybody who interferes with either is liable to be a patient of Guy's.

To board one of these buses was a gamble, for there was no certainty that it would call at regular stops or ever reach its supposed destination. Passengers were picked up at their convenience and if they lived off route or had caught the wrong bus, well, a detour could easily be arranged (p. 47), as could one to collect the girl friend or visit the club. If passen-gers objected to these irregularities they were chaffed as spoilsports and given stern lectures on the need for sacrifices during a national crisis. The drivers often lost their way, and

Pedestrian. "I'M AFRAID YOU'RE FULLY LOADED, AREN'T YOU?"
Owner-Driver. "NOT AT ALL, MADAM. THERE'S STILL ONE KNEE VACANT AT THE BACK, IF YOU DON'T MIND LETTING YOUR LEGS DANGLE OUTSIDE."

Punch 19 May 1926

as few of them were accustomed to heavy-duty driving the progress of their vehicles was often kangaroo-like and their accident rate very high.

The public tolerated the inefficiency and the practical jokes of the volunteers with good humour, half a loaf being better than no buses. If they found it all too much and wanted to boost morale they could always go and rub shoulders with an earl or two, or one of the many other titled gentlemen who had laid down their fly rods for the nation. The upper classes were obsessed with an urge for menial duties (p. 49), although one suspects their motives as so many of them landed jobs driving trains (p. 37). The society magazines were full of their photographs — on the footplate waving oil cans, beaming from signal boxes, blowing whistles and flapping flags, or staring with unbelieving indignation at the buffers they had just crashed the train into. The Honourable Lionel Guest drove a train between Liverpool Street and Yarmouth, Lord Weymouth also drove a train. Lord Monkwell operated the Marylebone signal box. Lord Portarlington worked as a porter at Paddington as did the Master of the Cambridge University Drag Hounds at Dover. But to enjoy the ultimate in high-class railway service it was necessary to take one of the infrequent trains to Westminster Underground Station — if you were lucky Beverley Nichols as Guard 4156 might be on board, which was being run by Conservative Members of Parliament. On alighting you would be welcomed by Stationmaster Lord Huntingfield (Eye Division), while Rail Foreman the Marquis of Tichfield (Newark) examined the coupling-joints; with luck your luggage would be borne away by Sir Victor Warrender (Grantham) and on leaving the station your ticket would be clipped by Major Ruggles-Brise (Malden).

Those with titles got most of the publicity, but the volunteers came from all classes and occupations. Accustomed to office work or teaching or living off dividends they found themselves unloading, driving, digging, greasing and carrying. At worst they worked long hours for little pay, ate hasty meals in open-air canteens, slept in blankets on the floor and braved the jeers and bricks of the strikers. Whatever their differences

Star 18 May 1926

in background they developed comradeship and unity as, amateurs all, they muddled and improvised their way through strange jobs, endured the same discomforts and developed the same pride. They were in one of those situations which the English look back on with sentiment and pride as being peculiarly their own, when impending disaster compels them into friendship and unity, when bungling and amateurishness somehow sees them through and when they discover for one glorious, brief moment that the people around them are human beings. If Dunkirk had not lain in the future its spirit would undoubtedly have been invoked (p. 59).

The public's good humoured response to the Strike and the light-hearted seriousness of the volunteers were celebrated as a uniquely British characteristic. If anyone deserved praise for these qualities it was surely the strikers, the majority of whom conducted themselves like Rotarians. The T.U.C. continually urged the strikers to keep within the law and strove to make the Strike as genteel as possible. The first bulletin to Strike Committees beautifully expressed its cosy, British assumptions: 'The General Council suggests that in all districts where large numbers of workmen are idle, sports should be organised and entertainments arranged. This will keep both a number of people busy and provide amusement for many more'. It was in this spirit, rather than one which encouraged the wrecking of buses, that the T.U.C. rallied its troops.

The Strike Committees were responsible for the lawful nature and orderliness of their activities and often won the admiration of the police for their discipline and control. In some areas they accepted responsiblity for general law and order and shepherded their marches and demonstrations through the streets, directing traffic, controlling crowds, breaking up fights, watched by an amused police force. In Lincoln the police asked the Trades Council to supply special constables, which it did, and in Newcastle strikers assisted the Civil Commissioner with unloading foodstuffs until stopped by the Government. Many strikers wore their war medals, which the *British Worker* believed impressed the

middle classes; it would certainly be difficult to overlook the irony that men who had fought for their country now had their country fighting them:

> Stand by the Country's Standard
> > And see the trouble through
> And when the war is over
> > Count on Us to stand by You.

With relatively few exceptions relations between police and strikers were good and each spent a lot of time praising the behaviour of the other (p. 53). In Brighton strikers presented the Chief Constable with a silver salver in appreciation of the restraint and understanding shown by his men, a gesture more meaningfully paralleled in Ashby-de-la-Zouch where the police started a fund for the starving families of three strikers who had been imprisoned for stealing chickens. And then there was that weird football match in Plymouth where the strikers beat the police 2-1. Perhaps it was despair at the indecency of the occasion which prompted the local news-paper's ambiguous headline 'Chief Constable's Wife Kicked Off'. There were literally thousands of these little incidents where police and strikers forgot that they were on opposing sides in a deadly industrial conflict and behaved as if they were in a cricket match. This was Britain in the grip of revolution; these were the revolutionaries of whom the government was demanding unconditional surrender.

If the strikers and the public seemed to take the crisis lightly this was not true of the government. With the Civil Commissioners at their posts and their plans efficiently functioning the struggle was transferred to the House of Commons and became one of words and psychology. On every possible occasion Government spokesmen made it their business to denounce the Strike as a direct threat to the Constitution and not a straightforward dispute between employers and workers. 'Constitutional government is being attacked', said Baldwin, 'the General Strike is a challenge to Parliament and is the road to anarchy and ruin'. This was partly true, as the Strike was no longer the concern of the coal

industry alone, but Baldwin well knew that the General Council was as staunchly constitutionalist as he and that its objective was the limited one of a settlement for the miners. The 'constitutional issue' was a sophisticated version of the 'revolutionary issue'.

When the T.U.C. had called out the 'first line' industries it had included the printers with these as a defensive measure against the overwhelmingly hostile press. This was a grave mistake, for most national newspapers ceased publication and the Government was enabled to dominate news and propaganda through the B.B.C. and through its own strike newspaper, the *British Gazette.* 'Don't forget the cleverest thing I ever did', Baldwin later told his official biographer. 'I put Winston in a corner and told him to edit the *British Gazette*'. Winston was not one to be kept long in a corner, and he soon came out breathing fire to give Baldwin many uncomfortable moments and the General Strike one of its most odious chapters. In Cabinet deliberations before the Strike Churchill had led the group which demanded a strong line against the T.U.C. and which had caused Baldwin, basically a peace-loving man, to embrace the doctrine of unconditional surrender. In current parlance Churchill was a hawk; the way he set about editing the *British Gazette* he should more accurately have been termed a wolf, and his prey on this occasion was the British striker. Many people, including some Conservative M.P.'s, thought that the Government's newspaper would be impartial in the dispute and would observe accepted journalistic standards. In this they overlooked the personality of Winston Churchill, for in his eyes, and he printed this, the strikers were 'the enemy' (p. 55) and the Strike 'a hold-up . . . a direct challenge to ordered government'. To Churchill 'the enemy' had only one connotation, and with typical vigour and ruthlessness, and bedammed to Fleet Street ethics, he set out to destroy it.

From its first headline to its last colophon the *British Gazette* was absolutely partial to the Government's case. With complete disregard for future industrial relations it attacked the

"THE BRITISH WORKER."

Mr. Punch (*to Volunteer*): "THANK YOU, SIR."

strikers in the most savage terms, and it seriously maintained that the T.U.C. was attempting to establish an alternative government, was making 'an effort to enforce upon some 42 million British citizens the will of less than four million others'. The Strike as reported by the *British Gazette* was a seriously compromised version of the truth; it printed exaggerated figures of the number of trains and buses which were running when the official, much lower ones, were known; it gave wide coverage to anti-strike speeches and ignored those in favour of compromise – even when made by the Archbishop of Canterbury; violence by strikers was meticulously detailed, that by the police ignored; incorrect or totally false reports of strikers returning to work were frequently printed, corrections supplied by the T.U.C. went into the wastepaper basket, and an utterly inaccurate picture of the Strike slowly collapsing was sedulously cultivated over several days.

The *Gazette* made statements in the name of the Government which had never been approved by the Cabinet, and one in particular which promised the Armed Forces the full support of the Government in 'any action which they may find it necessary to take in an honest endeavour to aid the Civil Power', was widely regarded as an incitement to violence, provoked a protest from the King and a denial from Baldwin. The *British Gazette* was one of the least salutary episodes in Churchill's career and contributed substantially to that intense dislike which the working class had for him. But for all its nastiness the *British Gazette* provided one of the best jokes of the Strike in its daily homily 'Many false rumours are current. Believe nothing until you see it in the *British Gazette*'.

The *British Gazette* was foreign to Baldwin's style of politics but it was saying in a crude manner the same as he was: that the strike notices must be withdrawn before the Government would enter into any negotiations. This policy began to attract more and more opposition as the Strike went on, but any waverings Baldwin may have felt would have been set at rest by Cardinal Bourne, preaching in Westminster Cathedral, when he declared that 'there is no moral

DITCHED!

JOHN BULL: "A bad smash, and it will cost a lot to repair."

The General Strike has dealt a serious blow to British trade at a moment when signs of revival were pronounced.

News of the World 16 May 1926

justification for this General Strike. It is a sin against the obedience we owe to God', adding for good measure that the Government 'represents in its own sphere the authority of God himself'. It was said that Churchill queried the 'represents'.

More seriously Sir John Simon, a respected laywer-M.P., speaking in the House of Commons on 6 May declared that the Strike was not, in legal terms, a strike at all but an illegal inducement to workers to break their contracts by a third party, and that the trade-union leaders concerned were 'liable in damages to the uttermost farthing of their personal possessions'. This judgment was later destroyed by other lawyers, and at the time the T.U.C. leaders received contrary advice and were not troubled by it, but Simon's statement worried many strikers and had a strong impact on public opinion. The *British Gazette* made much of it and it probably lay behind the tougher policy which the Government followed from then on over striker's pay and in the London Docks.

The London Docks had proved to be a stronghold for the T.U.C. and only 40 out of 14,000 dockers were at work. The Government had solved the immediate problem there of maintaining electricity for the massive refrigeration plants by the brilliant expedient of connecting them to the generators of submarines in the River Thames. The second problem was to unload the ships and transport food into London through the heavily picketed dock gates. On 6 May the Cabinet decided to make an issue of the blockage on the Docks, partly to obtain food for London and partly as a show of strength. After darkness that night they floated barges filled with volunteers down river to the Docks and at the same time moved in armed detachments of Bluejackets and Grenadier Guardsmen to guard the Gates. When dawn came the astonished pickets were presented with a *fait accompli* of troops guarding the Gates on the outside and volunteers unloading ships on the inside. By dawn on 8 May over 100 lorries had been loaded with food, and guarded by Welsh and Coldstream Guardsmen and with an armoured car escort

THE STRIKER'S RETURN.

Employer. "GLAD TO SEE YOU BACK, MY LAD; BUT YOU'LL UNDERSTAND THAT IN THE CIRCUMSTANCES WE CAN'T RUN TO A FATTED CALF."

from the Royal Tank Corps, they made a triumphal procession through cheering crowds to the Hyde Park Food Depot. The blockade on the London Docks had been broken and the Government had shown that it was prepared to threaten the use of force.

The episode of the striker's pay was another example of the Government becoming less passive in its attitude to the Strike, although on this occasion it had no success. The Government decided on 11 May to introduce a Bill which would make it illegal for trade-union funds to be in any way used for strike purposes, and as an interim measure issued an Order in Council prohibiting banks from paying money to anyone 'acting against the national interest'. King George V, who was much distressed by the Strike and who had a liberalising influence on the Cabinet — the strikers 'are my people as well' — protested to the Home Secretary against 'anything done to touch the pockets of those who are now only existing on strike pay'. The proposal was dropped, but the lesson did not go unlearned on the General Council, which was beginning to appreciate the immense powers which a determined government could command.

At T.U.C. Headquarters the first week saw the Strike Organisation Committee obtain firm control over activities in the country. Adequate communications had been established with Strike Committees which were keeping Headquarters in touch with developments in its own and Government spheres; the Committees were controlling the Strike very capably and were not generally seeking too much independence; while a newspaper, the *British Worker*, had been established as a rather feeble reply to the *British Gazette*, which removed the need for local Committees to print their own, possibly radical, papers. The S.O.C. was still overwhelmed by the flood of delegates, requests for instructions and requests for the clarification of instructions, and there was the problem of preventing other over-enthusiastic unions from joining the Strike; but the Strike was mostly under control and confidence and morale in the field were

The Miner 25 September 1926

extremely high. During the week the General Council had continued its policy of seeking a negotiated settlement with the Government and several members had met with prominent politicians and business men to try and find a basis for a compromise. Response to the Strike had been splendid, but after a week it was obvious to the Council that the country was, with difficulty, continuing to function. The strikers and the Government had reached an impasse which seemed likely to continue for several weeks and which might be beyond the resources of their limited strike funds. Time would increase the likelihood of violence and serious clashes with the authorities, and this they were against at any price. There were rumours that weekend that the Government was preparing to arrest the strike leaders and seize union funds and these, whether true or false, increased their awareness of the Government's power if it decided to launch an all-out attempt to break the Strike, instead of more or less tolerating it. Faced with these pressures in circumstances which many of them were opposed to anyhow, they quietly decided that the time had come to call off the Strike, assuming that a suitable opportunity for an honourable settlement presented itself. A suitable opportunity in the person of Sir Herbert Samuel of Coal Commission fame did present itself.

Samuel had made an early offer to the Government of his services as a mediator in the Strike and when this had been rejected he had retired to Italy to write a philosophical book. On 6 May he had returned to England, still wishing to ameliorate the consequences of his own Report, and through J. H. Thomas had been put in touch with the General Council's Negotiating Committee. He had also had dealings with the Cabinet which, although most sympathetic to his objectives, had emphasised most strongly that any proposals which he might 'agree' with the General Council could not have 'any vestige of official character' – it would like to see a settlement but wanted no part in any negotiations.

Throughout the weekend of 8 May Samuel, Thomas and the Negotiating Committee met secretly to devise terms on

" While the miners are our enemies we should not feed them. We did not feed the Germans, and I cannot for the life of me see why we should feed the miners."—Lord Hunsdon.

which a settlement could be made. The Miners' leaders knew nothing of these meetings, nor any of the strikers whom the General Council was that weekend urging to stand firm. The deliberations produced a document, subsequently known as the Samuel Memorandum, which proposed a package in which the Strike would be called off, the owners would withdraw the lock-out notices, any discussion on reducing miner's wages would be deferred until specific proposals for re-organising the coal industry had been drawn up and a National Mines Board would be set up to deal with disputes in the industry and to supervise its re-organisaton. This was the Samuel Report with the re-organisation of the industry a condition of, rather than a consequence of, any reduction in wages. It was not until Sunday, 9 May, when the proposals were fairly precise, that Smith and Cook, the Miners' leaders, were acquainted with them. Both rejected them out of hand as they implied the possibility of a reduction in wages. Smith and Cook were deeply angered at having been excluded from the discussions until they were almost complete, and fears were aroused of a double-cross by the T.U.C. Any discussions which included J. H. Thomas aroused these fears in them. The Simon Memorandum was accepted by the General Council and for the next four days the scenes preceding the Strike were repeated, except that an immovable Government was replaced by an immovable Miners' Federation. Smith and Cook were as stubborn as Baldwin, although for better reasons; they reiterated their objections to the Memorandum and demanded to know what guarantees the General Council had that the Government would accept it *after* the Strike had been called off.

The members of the General Council met with the Miners' Federation on the assumption that any decision on the Memorandum lay with them and not with the Miners. On 1 May unions had handed over their powers in the Strike to the T.U.C., and having assumed responsibility for starting the Strike the T.U.C. was also entitled to terminate it. The Miners' Federation was only one union among many; the others had made sacrifices for the miners – the T.U.C. was now asking the miners to make sacrifices for them. When Smith and Cook rejected this interpretation of 1 May the General Council, believing that the Memorandum was the best settlement they would ever get, reluctantly decided to call off the Strike in spite of the opposition of the Miners' Federation. At this stage Bevin closely questioned the Negotiating Committee if the lock-out notices would be withdrawn and the Memorandum accepted by the Government if the Strike was called off. He was answered 'yes' on both points. Bevin also received an assurance that the men returning to work would be safeguarded against victimisation. In the morning of Wednesday, 12 May, Bevin called at the Miners' Federation Office with some colleagues to make a last plea for agreement and unity but his efforts were rejected. He took a cab to Downing Street to join the Negotiating Committee which had arranged to meet Baldwin at noon, a Baldwin who already knew that the General Council and the Miners' Federation were split. When they entered Number 10 a Permanent Secretary asked them their business. 'We want to see the Prime Minister' he was told. 'You know the Prime Minister will not see you before the Strike is called off'. From the back Bevin cried 'For Christ's sake let's call it on again if this is the position'. Thomas stepped forward and said 'We have come to call the Strike off'.

SURRENDER OF THE REVOLUTIONARIES was the *Daily Mail's* triumphant headline the next day, while the *British Gazette* cried 'Unconditional withdrawal of Notice by T.U.C.'. On the previous evening in a B.B.C. broadcast Baldwin had likewise said that the Strike had been ended 'without conditions entered into by the Government'. This was the awful truth: the Strike had been called off without any guarantee that the Government would accept the Samuel Memorandum, without any guarantee that the owners would withdraw the lock-out notices or that strikers would not be victimised. The General Council had been out-manoeuvred or had been incredibly naive. It was surrender and it was unconditional.

The news of the Strike being called off was received by the

strikers with incredulity. The day before the 'second line' industries had been called out in a show of confidence and the *British Worker* had celebrated the strength and firmness of the strikers. The B.B.C.'s 1 p.m. news bulletin 'General Strike ceases today' threw everyone into confusion, and it was widely assumed that it signified victory for the General Council. Meetings were held and leaflets distributed glorifying this and in some districts 'Victory' editions of strike bulletins were printed. Even when later news bulletins and Baldwin's broadcast proved that this was the opposite of the truth there was widespread disbelief. A trick was suspected or a plot to save the Government's face. Anything seemed possible except the truth. As the real implications of the surrender dawned bewilderment gave way to fury. Telegrams and protests deluged T.U.C. Headquarters attacking and denouncing the capitulation. 'An inglorious and humiliating surrender', wired the Amalgamated Society of Woodworkers, 'one of the most deplorable and discreditable episodes in the history of the trade unions'. 'Alarm – fear – despair – a victorious army disarmed and handed over to its enemies' said the Hull Strike Committee. These were typical of the reactions of ordinary strikers, and their anger increased when the B.B.C. announced that Cook had instructed the miners not to return to work. The General Council publicly maintained that it had received assurances for a settlement on the lines of the Samuel Memorandum, but the Government denied that it had given them. The assurances had come from Samuel and Thomas on the basis of nods and winks from those close to Baldwin; they were worthless.

As if to prove to the General Council just how steadfast the strikers had been there grew from their anger one of the most remarkable episodes of the Strike – the Second General Strike. Workers returning to their jobs on 13 May found that many employers refused to take them on or else penalised them by reducing wages, demoting them or demanding that they give up trade union membership. This victimisation (p. 63) was very common, particularly on the railways. As the General Council had not obtained from the Government any

Visitor. "YOUR SON IS LOOKING VERY BORED."
Fond Mother. "YES. YOU SEE, HE MISSES THE STRIKE SO DREADFULLY."

Punch 2 June 1926

protection for these workers it seemed that many employers were determined to extract the maximum number of fruits from their victory. In reaction to this there grew up at Strike Committee level a spontaneous rejection of the General Council's instructions in the form of a determination to remain on strike. This was the sullen, belligerent reaction of men who refused to be beaten, and they were joined in this by workers from other industries. On the day after the Strike was officially called off the number on strike increased by

100,000. This provoked national alarm, the matter was raised in the House of Commons and Baldwin was forced to condemn victimisation of any kind. This was the only concession to be won from the Strike.

Thus ended the General Strike with defeat for the T.U.C. and the strikers. Nothing tangible had been gained, a great deal had been lost. Many strikers *were* victimised and some were never to work again. The unions had lost a great deal of money, which with a drop in membership to pre-1916 numbers was to weaken their influence for a decade. Only the Government could derive any satisfaction from the result, and it celebrated its victory by a Trades Disputes Act, which in addition to severely restricting all strikes, made illegal the calling of another general strike.

The miners battled on for another seven months, when there were still 800,000 on strike. Their position was absolutely hopeless but they refused to recognise this. Baldwin abandoned the Samuel Commission proposals and offered less generous ones of his own, then abandoned these and left negotiations entirely to the owners (p. 65). Abject poverty and starvation was commonplace in the coal fields and in some districts miner's families were denied public assistance because the miner 'had freely chosen to be unemployed' (p. 67). A Miner's Relief Fund was started by the Mayor of London. Still they held out, 'the heroism outweighing the stupidity'. At the end of November they could continue no longer : funds were exhausted and the strike was beginning to weaken in some areas. They gave in, accepted the owner's terms and returned to work for reduced wages, longer hours and without a national minimum or a national agreement. The terms, in fact, demanded in the lock-out notices on 'Red Friday' sixteen heroic months earlier.